dear younger self

AN ANTHOLOGY TO INSPIRE SELF-REFLECTION

BY SUSAN LOWENTHAL AXELROD

Dear Younger Self:
An Anthology to Inspire Self-Reflection

ISBN: 978-0-578-68652-3

First Edition - May 2020

Copyright © 2020 by Susan Lowenthal Axelrod

All rights reserved. No part of this book may be reproduced in any form without written permission from the copyright holder.

Published by JGU Press. Printed in the USA.

Design & Layout by Carasmatic Design - www.CarasmaticDesign.com

CONTENTS

Preface 6

Introduction 8

1. Dear Younger Self 10

2. Getting Okay With Awkward 14

3. Are You Ready? 18

4. What If I Succeed? 22

5. How Does This Serve Me? 26

6. Turn Towards Instead of Away 30

7. Who Were You Then? 34

8. Discovering You Again 38

9. Stepping Out 42

10. My Well-Being, My Responsibility 46

11. I am Enough 50

12. I am a Healer 53

13. Something Big is Coming 57

14. The Army of Change 61

15. Get Control of Your Mind 65

16. Your Soul, Uniquely Yours 69

17. Let Go 73

18. Bonus Meditation: Soul Rising 77

Conclusion: Self Reflections, What Now? 80

PREFACE

Is it that simple?

Can you really just create a book from a body of work you've already created?

Turns out, it is and you can.

I have been surprised (an understatement) at the response to my first 'little' book that I titled, *Your Job Is To Be*. Here are just a few comments people have shared with me: "I keep this book in my purse!" "It's by my bedside for when I need positive inspiration before I sleep." "I love the writing pages, they help me process my thoughts." The whole thing happened in such an extraordinary way, in two weeks from the idea to full manuscript upload on Amazon. There was something magical about it. But, was it magic, really?

It was not magic. It was passion, commitment, giving, time, work, tears, sharing, growing and deepest desire to help another and create my own legacy. That's the truth. The story of how my first book came to *Be* (see what I did there?!) traverses a seventeen-month period of writing soul-inspired articles for *Luminous*

Wisdom | Sophia—a global online magazine of Sibella Publications & Sibella Circle International—plus several years in friendship and partnership with Nechama Laber co-creating the foundation of a global online community for Jewish girls called Jewish Girls Unite. We founded JGU Press as one revenue source to create a sustainable organization to support our Jewish daughters.

So, the Independent Press existed and I was writing for the magazine and that's when the 'magic' happened, worlds collided and the synergistic outcome for me was my book. I had begun to think that publishing a book was just a dream that would never be achieved. But doing the work (writing and submitting monthly articles, no matter what) and working in a mutually synergistic way with a partner (especially when you're giving from the heart) helped me realize a long-held goal.

The response I have received from readers has been the mortar that has bonded my commitment to keep writing. If you have a long-held dream, I say: Dream On! And, get to work, our world needs to hear the message in you.

INTRODUCTION

On Self-Reflecting

Dear Reader,

Is self-reflection too 'all about me'?

I say nay.

If we can become more consciously aware of our thoughts, ask ourselves activating questions, and then give ourselves the gift of getting quiet and listening, our self-reflection can offer the answers we so desperately seek to live the life we imagine. Through my own life—a treacherous journey at times—and through my work as a coach for women in the second-half of life, I've learned that most of us have deeply personal thoughts, wishes and dreams. And, that most of us don't believe that we will ever achieve our deepest desires.

The articles in this book offer you permission to dream. Each offers you the opportunity to reflect on your own life, how you've lived in the past, who you are now and who you want to be. At every age, you have 1,440 minutes each and every day to *live*.

Of course, we do not know how many more days or minutes we have. I want to encourage, inspire and motivate you to do anything that you need to do in order to use the time as you want. Not in the way that others want, or that you feel you *should*. This is the time of life that can be yours, if you realize the opportunity.

What's that you say? You're still caring for or responsible to others? Of course you are; we're women, it's what we do. I'm just suggesting that you reformulate the way you see yourself, your time, the day, your obligations/commitments/responsibilities, and that you prioritize yourself a bit higher now than you have in the past. Why? Because your soul is crying out for this. She's feeling stifled and stymied. You prioritizing yourself higher on this list at this time of *your* life will give *her* life.

I hope the articles and writing pages in this book will offer you the time you need to self-reflect and soul-connect. And, by all means, share your thoughts with others! Discuss! Converse. Your soul will thank you. When you turn life's experiences into wisdom and then share your wisdom with others, you will find relevance and meaning in your life beyond which you can imagine. I am 100% certain that you will find positive resonance in these pages to help you self-reflect. Enjoy!

Wishing you the best always,

Susan

1

DEAR YOUNGER SELF

Dear Younger Self: Appreciate the sun and the moon, the tides and the sand, the rain and the wind. And your breath. Appreciate your breath more. These are the markers of life. Material things are nice, they are not unimportant. But in the end, when things get so hard that you think you cannot bear it, there is one thing that you can still rely on—the earth will rotate, dawn will arrive. So, make more time to sit in nature and breathe, just breathe. Feel your breath connecting to the essence of the earth, the tone of the tides, or the majesty of the mountains. Please know that it is ok to believe in God as the universal source of all that is. But, know, too that it is free will and choice that is your connection to Self. This connection will support you throughout the perilous journey that is one's life.

From the moment you become a sentient human, there is a question that you begin to ask yourself that never goes away: "Am I ok?" It becomes gradient, taking on mass proportions in later years. The "Am I going to fall?" thought you might have from learning to walk turns into "Am I going to fail?" about, well, everything throughout the stages of life. There is a glory-time when girls hit a power-stride at about age 6 or 7; "I CAN" exudes, "I WILL" comes forth, "I AM" lasts for another few years. Take a moment now to breathe, reflect and try to connect to your inner 8-year-old—she's in there; what do you remember about her? Give yourself over to her fearlessness for a moment. Breathe.

What happened to that girl? Many things, each one acting like a relentless sledgehammer pounding her down: advertising, puberty, Mean Girls, boys, lack of strong women role models, self-questioning, Good-Girl syndrome. She was gloriously internal for her developing earliest years, so many thoughts within; everything was a wonder. But exposure to life brought her outward, to the external self that would be thrashed about for decades, often ending up like a wet rag on the floor. Hyperbole? No. Reality.

To that self I want to say: Honeypie, know, just know that there will be a time that you come into your own. If not sooner perhaps, then when you reach your late-middle age years, there is a freedom the likes of which you cannot imagine now. There appears to be some

There is a freedom the likes of which you cannot imagine now. magic about aging into this stage if you allow it. Perhaps it's from the self-knowledge of: "DID IT" [often followed by "Don't know how well, but at least it's done"]. Whether it's the launch of your children or for those with no children, the launch from later-career success, turning 50 can bring the beginning of an awareness that grows and grows. 60 [as I observe] can bring the liberation of breaking through. There is that last filmy layer, diaphanously fluttering in front of you, inviting you to step through, to see your old friends again! Hello! There in front of you in clear opulent vision are the sun, the moon, the trees, mountains and tides. Wow, breathe *that* in! And, breathe again quietly.

Coming into your own. Can it happen sooner? Yes! It can! If you want it, if you figure out what that means to you. If you give yourself permission, and if you allow it. What *does* it mean to you? Connect back to *your* source, not to the material things, not to the success that others project. Go in, go deep. Come into your own, now.

self-reflections

GETTING OKAY WITH AWKWARD

I feel awkward sometimes. This surprises me because I have been a confident person and woman since I was approximately 15 years old. I have examined that self-confidence, where did it come from? Surely the privilege of growing up in a loving, supportive, highly educated, faith-based household created a strong foundation for me.

I am aware of the privilege of attending good schools, summer camp, leadership training programs, supplemental educational programs, a best college and having financial security. Stealthily, confidence crept in and lasted for decades. Of course, I had doubts and downers over the years, but I faced them with a sense of knowing that I would get through to the other side.

Now, suddenly, at this stage of life, I feel awkward. I

am just older than Young. I am way younger than Old, but I see it on my Horizon. I feel it coming with each passing day, sometimes showing itself through a foggy thought, sometimes an ache or a pain, or sometimes a deep sadness for the eventuality of leaving our world. And always, there is an awareness of time passing quickly.

I see myself through different eyes today. But what is it that I see? The answer is that I don't know. And that is what makes me feel awkward. Who is this middle-aged person? Is she OK? What is her future? I breathe.

And then, suddenly, alignment. I remember that her future is now; this moment, this day, this offering, this impact. Maturity and resulting commitment to self ensures that I am on-point, on purpose, on-target to meet my goals. All of my goals lead to just one thing: being comfortable in my own skin. Is this something you struggle with? Do you wonder who the person is you see in the mirror, or in your mind's eye? Is she on track in life, now?

To get on track, use breathing, meditation, prayer, tools—whatever it takes to breathe easily In This Moment. Ah, that definitely feels better. I do this. A reminder that it is in my control at any moment to take a breath, visit with my thoughts and move easily through awkwardness to ease In This Moment. Ease

I see myself through different eyes today.

then leads to calm and I am back on the right path. Will I get triggered again with awkward moments, with doubt, with fear or sadness? I will. And when I do, I will Breathe Again and again if necessary, sit in the feeling-moment allowing it to be what it is, and move gracefully through to self-awareness again. This is self-leadership; I invite you to become a Self- Leadership Master. It will serve you to help you get okay with awkward.

self-reflections

3

ARE YOU READY?

What is it that is on your mind that you want, want to have, or want to do?

Whatever it is, are you ready for it? Are you ready to receive it, to accomplish it, to feel it, to see it? Or, are you only seeing it as a *wish* or a *dream*? Something that you 'would love' or 'would do if you won the lottery,' or 'only happens for others, but not me'? If this is the case, I encourage you to imagine the possibilities.

Imagine the possibility that the thing in your mind could happen...for you. Just imagine. It's possible, it's possible; yes, it's possible. I know this because it happened to me. When I went from needing to have it all right now, to figuring out what was truly important and letting go of the other [expectations of self that were imprinted from legacy, society or anyone else at all], plus allowing time to be my friend [instead of my imposing/pending enemy], and then bringing structure to my desire, things started happening that were exactly as I had dreamed or imagined.

Often, we imagine things to be impossible because we have not brought structure to the thought, and whatever it is, we want it all and we want it now. If you open your mind to the possibility that this 'thing' could be yours if you plan for it, incrementally, over time, then you can have it/achieve it/do it.

If, with intention and commitment, you move the idea from dream to possibility, what might that look like, what would it take? Exactly, precisely, what structure and what steps would it take for you to achieve the dream if you planned for it?

If you were highly intent on running a race, would you simply show up on race day and expect to be in the best shape? Not likely. You would plan for a course of training over a period of time to make sure your body was in shape, and your stamina was high enough to compete. If you were entering a cooking contest, would you show up without the exact right ingredients, having tested and tried the recipe repeatedly?

Adopt this mindset! Look that thing you want straight in the eye and imagine it in hi-resolution.

Just imagine. It's possible, it's possible; yes, it's possible.

When you do this, you may realize that you should 'be careful what you wish for!' Or, you may affirm to yourself, "I want that." And, set an intention, commit to it, make a plan and practice/train/re-imagine on the way to achieving or obtaining this thing.

Finally, be sure that you see what is right in front of you! You may not even realize that parts or pieces are falling into place in front of your eyes! One day, as happened to me, you'll be launching your signature workshop in Sedona, AZ!

self-reflections

4

WHAT IF I SUCCEED?

Fear of failure, the most human of concerns. "What if I fail?" "What if it doesn't work?" "What if I can't do it?" Are these the thoughts that you give space to in your head? Have you found that you are not willing to try something for fear of failing? "Who am I to do this?" "I don't even know how." "It probably won't work."

Can you feel that? The rumination of negative thoughts and energy that you permit to wash over you and disallow your potential. Full reveal here, this has been me more times than I care to admit. Harder yet, because I am a Coach who helps women get clear and confident to live life in a more calm, comfortable in their own skin and connected to self-energy.

However, even as I have these doubting thoughts, I have a deeper knowing: I'm on the right path. How do I know? Because to be my most authentic self, and offer my best service to my clients, I spend a great amount of time reflecting, thinking deeply, planning for and envisioning their best success...which comes from my best success. My deep knowing offers me relief and comfort. And, my clients tell me that I help them, they thank me, they tell me they are so grateful; some even tell me "I love you."

Still, fear of failure shows her mean face to me sometimes. Why don't I believe my clients? Do I think they're lying? Why do I believe 'fear of failure?' In the frequent alone-time I have as a Coach, either in my office or while walking Mr. Cooper to expend his crazy dog-energy, I Breathe, Open, Allow and Think [my 'B.O.A.T.' meditation!] and ask myself this: *So, what if I fail?* What does it mean if I do? What would happen? In my mature middle years, having spent a decade of exploration and commitment to enlightened self-love, I know that there is no failure. Not even spectacular ones. There is only trial-and-error; try, try-again; start/stop-start/stop; but all the while, keep putting one foot in front of the other, breathe and know that I'm on the right path, my path.

These days, I ask myself a different question: What if I succeed? When I ask that, usually I have a subtle breath-intake and shudder, fear again? Oh my, what if I succeed? What if I succeed in a big way? What then? Would I be revealed, my secret out? What if my message

What if I succeed in a big way?

of self-love and acceptance leaks out to millions? Or, what if just one person—the exact person who needs to hear it—receives my message and believes? Like the sobbing mother of the murdered adult son whom I met on a bus and spoke with...two years later she called me again because I had helped her feel better in that moment. What if I fail?

Really? NO! ...WHAT IF I SUCCEED?

self-reflections

5

HOW DOES THIS SERVE ME?

In the wisdom of my maturing years, I have identified a question that changes my worried nature. 'How does this serve me?' So many things over the years would have been different if I had known to ask myself this question.

Yet, is it all about me? Does everything have to serve me? In a way, yes. It is all about me. If I am worried, anxious, nervous, afraid or anything on the negative side of the feelings scale, then that emanates outwardly from me to everyone in my existence and everything I touch. If I am on the positive side of the feelings scale anything from okay to elation, then that is what emanates outwardly from me. Most of us are familiar with the phrase 'if momma's happy, we're all happy' or 'happy wife, happy life.' The single question 'how does this serve me?' helps to get me better able to create the good space in which I want to hang out.

'How does this serve me?' If I ask the question and take a breath, and open to see if I am connected to my self-energy, the energy that is also connected to God, the universal source of all that is, then I often find the answer I am seeking. 'How does this serve me?' It serves me to be okay, to be good, to be connected to self and to the impact I want to make in the world. If I sense the answer 'it doesn't serve me!' as in: it doesn't serve well to be who and how I want to be, it doesn't help me be clear, calm and on purpose right now, then I breathe again and allow it to move through me and float away. Or, sometimes I kick its ass out of me. Negativity does not get to take up space in my mind and heart, twisting my mood and emotions and taking a toll on my wellbeing.

How did I get to this mature way of thinking? Because I lived the opposite for two of my life decades in which I created marriage+children=family. I suffer a bit for not having known the power of this simple question then. Might I have been less yelling-mom? Role modeling for our daughters the opportunity to take responsibility for one's emotions/frame of mind and behavior? And teaching-by-example that when you take responsibility for your own self/feelings/emotions, then you get control of same! And role modeling better wife responsibilities, stopping the blame game. 'How does this serve me?' 'What's in my

What if I take control of my thoughts here and now, this moment?

life?' 'What if I take control of my thoughts here and now, this moment?' 'What if I do what is in my control to change the way I'm feeling or thinking, take responsibility to transform and shift this mindset I'm in right now?'

How does this serve me? A simple question to change your life.

self-reflections

6

TURN TOWARDS INSTEAD OF AWAY

Two words can change your life. If you seek change, if you desperately want something different, I encourage you to realize the power of a Power Phrase.

For years, I was desperately seeking something in my marriage. I thought I could explain it in words. But in the end, and after much work, I realized that what I wanted was to feel something. I had put the responsibility of this in my husband's hands. I saw myself through his eyes and I experienced life in the way that I thought he experienced life [I was wrong]. I took a long journey to move towards 'Being'—for myself, by myself, with myself; getting quiet and going in. I found and accepted my responsibility for my own life. And, surprise! I found and felt more control!

Over the years, I lapsed periodically. One of these times ended up in a bad fight with my husband after which I told him—again—we needed to go to counseling [something he had always refused]. Shockingly, he agreed. His soul, too, must have been yearning to feel better with me, no? I was the one who took responsibility to figure it out. The old me would have spent time resenting that. The new me was filled with gratitude that we were going.

Two busy professionals, I couldn't find a good time. I got creative and looked for marriage counseling retreats. I found one on karma sutra, but he wasn't exactly comfortable with that! I continued to search. And I found a Gottman weekend retreat. I knew this was exactly right because Dr. John Gottman's book, The Seven Principles for Making Marriage Work, had already played a role in my personal transformation regarding our marriage. Magically, we were both available for that weekend. The short story was that we arrived with open hearts, both ready to commit and do the work to feel better together. It became clear that we were already *Masters* in our relationship and that we were doing just fine. It was all quite remarkable. But there was *one key lesson* I still use to this day, the Power Phrase 'Turn Towards.' If you're feeling badly about something with your mate *or anyone*, try opening your heart and turning towards him or her. That's all, the simplest thing in the world: "Turn towards instead of

What if I take control of my thoughts here and now, this moment?

away."

Here are the elements that I've added to turn these words into a power phrase: come to conscious awareness of your thoughts, ask yourself "How do I *want* to feel right now?", breathe, open your heart, take responsibility for your feelings...for who you want to be and how you want to be. Then, *Turn Towards* your mate [or whomever *you want* to love].

Can you apply this? Mostly our hearts are closed through busyness, anger, resentment, sadness, loneliness, anxiety or fear. Take responsibility, open your heart and Turn Towards the person you want to love.

self-reflections

7

WHO WERE YOU THEN?

Do you ever take time to think of your old self, the person you were many years ago? Mostly, we live our lives day-to-day and even work to be mindfully present. We learn the benefit of being in the Here and Now, clearing your mind and bringing it to this moment so that you can move into the next moment from this place, this space, peacefully and with ease. Yet when opportunity presents itself to remember the old you, it can be helpful to take advantage and ask yourself who was I then? And who am I now? Opportunities to connect to your former self abound. When you go home for a holiday, go to a high school or college reunion, hear from someone you grew up with, drive-through a place that is reminiscent for you, there are many times that you might be presented with the opportunity to ask yourself: Who was I then? And who am I now?

At my 35th College reunion, we stayed in the dorm that I lived in my freshman year, 39 years prior. Who was I? The 18-year-old girl who drove up with her parents to be let off and start a new phase, a new life no longer under the watchful loving eye of parents who provided a safe and privileged space in which to grow. Who was that young person, what was she thinking and feeling, what did she think she would become? And now, 39 years later, who is this middle-aged woman driving up with her own thoughts about the life that became the reality of that 18-year-old girl. Who am I now? What has my life become, how have I been, how did it all go to this point, am I okay? Am I happy?

And further still. Walking the campus and seeing other women, older women attending their 45th, 55th, even 60th reunion, who will I be then? How will my life go over the next 10, 20, 30 or more years? There is more freedom to be comfortable in your own skin, flexibility because you have spent the time and done the work. Now is a time to discover you again. Who was I then? Who am I now? Who will I be? The choice is yours. The opportunity is yours. The time is now. Open your mind and imagine the possibilities that could be yours if you learn to breathe, clear your mind and get quiet, ask yourself who do I want to be and how do I want to be, and perhaps take a risk. What

Who was I then?
Who am I now?
Who will I be?

might you regret if you don't take a risk now? What might you risk if you live only with your regrets now?

Who was I then? Who am I now? Who will I be? The choice is yours, imagine the possibilities and take the risk! Enjoy!

self-reflections

8

DISCOVERING YOU AGAIN

Who am I in this new phase of life, a phase where I have more time and resources to be who I want to be and how I want to be? Who is that? What does it look like? What does it feel like?

'Discovering you again' is a process that allows personal growth, spiritual renewal, physical acceptance, and emotional calm. Are you interested in this new way of being? Are you ready to open and allow the possibility that you could feel comfortable in your own skin, confident in your skills and happy in your relationships? What will it take to become aware of the opening presenting itself to you? What will it take to discover you again?

Moving out of resistance to aging has been such a relief for me. It took well into my 50s but as I have worked to move into alignment with my age and stage, I have found grace and contentment that is a surprise for me.

On an intentional personal journey to find calm and reduce anxiety in my life, I learned about the idea that thoughts are things, that you can control and transform your thoughts, I found ease and enlightenment. I went into therapy, hired a coach, and committed to my physical body and mental well-being. All of this brought me further ease and helped me learn about the person I was becoming in this new stage of life.

My most significant realization was that the years of being an age that felt foreign, would also bring freedom and flexibility that I had not known for decades. The dawning of that age found me open and ready to discover myself again! I learned of the beauty of committing to this every day. I created tools for myself and now use these tools in my work as a coach to help other women realize their own potential, and the beauty and grace of having an inspired and impassioned second half.

Discovering you again! Who are you now? Who do you want to be now? How do you want to live? What matters to you? What is deeply meaningful in your life,

Dream, imagine, think, engage, act.

what inspires you,
what intrigues you,
what infuriates you and
what will you do about all of this?

I urge you to find tools to support your own thoughts and feelings—meditate, pray, sing, run, write! Discovering you again! There is joy to be found, there is ease and there is inspiration the likes of which you did not have time to imagine as your earlier self. Give yourself the gift of letting go of the old 'shoulds.' Ask yourself, what *could* I do? And be sure to bring structure in order to accomplish that which you are inspired to do. Find others who care, it's easier and more fun. Dream, imagine, think, engage, act. Our world desperately needs your skills and your passion. Live an inspired second half and leave behind a meaningful legacy.

self-reflections

9

STEPPING OUT

Is it time for me to do this? Isn't it too late, at the older side of middle-age, to step out into the spotlight? Or, is now the exact time? Exactly the time for me, for my family, for those who would hear me and for our world? Is it your time, too?

Every step I have taken has led me to this time, this moment. And you, every step you have taken has brought you exactly here. How does one do it? Step into the biggest moment of your life? I say 'life' not 'business' because the world I have created for myself is integrated. Life, work, play; play, work, life—it is all in a day for me. When better, then? When calm integration has sunk in, when purpose and focus mesh; when the very spirits themselves whisper into my ear: "I speak through you." It is time to step out, out of the comfort zone, out of the space of least resistance.

Into what? Into community? Into the world? The sky? No, it's the ether. It's the ether; the atmosphere, the very air we breathe. When you find your clearest breath, it goes all the way down to your toes, it shoots down further anchoring in the earth, firmly planted—implanted really—to ground you as you step out. What is the expression? 'Leap and the net shall appear'? Yes! It feels like stepping out onto the air and believing, knowing that the earth will rise to meet your foot. There is no alternative, you must step out, mindset transformed!

You tried staying in, staying in your small, cramped space; the Yearning crouched down deep inside you, hidden from the light. But she grew impatient, she kept trying to stretch and felt the bubble keeping her encased. She sat back and thought, "Maybe my place is here, maybe I should stay quiet here." But no! No, she threw up her arms, she stretched more and more, as far out as she could and she broke through the bubble. No longer encased, she rose floating up and out, gasping for air. Free, mindset transformed, life forever changed. It is time to Step Out.

She is you; you are now, it is time. Time to step out. It is her time, it is your time, it is our time. The world needs each of us to find our voice, *to allow our deepest Yearning to break free and make the impact we are destined to make with the Divine gifts given us.* Is there anything else? Could there be anything else? Yes,

It is time to Step Out.

there could be silence, suffering, yearning deep within; there could be life mildly lived, joy diminished, love scorned.

Or, there could be ecstasy! A clear breath, an easy mind, a joy-filled state of being and soul-connection with those in the orbit around you. Choose this. Step out.

self-reflections

10

MY WELL-BEING, MY RESPONSIBILITY

How many years did I put my own well-being in the hands of others? My parents, my husband, my boss, friends, even at times my children. I complained about so much. I railed out, I felt worried and then anxious, sad and then depressed.

Even as I acted out, I hated myself for being that way. When anyone told me to relax, I had a fit, a literal fit. Or sometimes, I felt such rage I would get very quiet, squint my eyes, lower my voice and say, "Don't tell me to relax." In those moments, I felt almost possessed. Today, I know it was my soul. She was so hurt, she was doing the best she could but always, to her, it was never enough. She tried and tried, she tried harder and harder but it just never seemed to be good enough. She suffered and shriveled. She felt alone and did not know what to do.

In those days, I knew nothing about self-love or breathing, indeed I mocked these things refusing to believe there could be substance there. Then, I had no idea that these were tools that could change my life.

Today, after a journey of nearly two decades, I have Tools that I use daily for myself and with my clients. Today, I teach the opportunity for finding control over your own life by taking responsibility for your well-being. When you take responsibility for your own well-being, your choices and your actions, things are 100% in your control (corollary: when you put your well-being into anyone else's hands, you feel out of control).

Look at the different areas of your life, go in and explore. We are multifaceted beings, take time to review and assess how you are doing in the many areas of your life—personal, spiritual, health, family, fun, career. When you do this, you will feel the experience of being responsible for your own well-being. You will be in charge; you will be in control. Think about well-being as an adjective, as in 'a well-being day.' Ask yourself, "What kind of well-being day am I having today?" Try to create a habit of asking yourself this question three times daily. You can also focus on a certain area as in, "What kind of spiritual well-being day am I having today?" If you answer that you are

Your soul will dance and sing.

having a mediocre or bad spiritual well-being day, then ask yourself, "What can I do right now to raise my spiritual well-being?"

When you come to awareness about your well-being feeling, you bring control to life in the way you have always sought. Practice, practice, practice. Do whatever you need to create the habit of asking yourself about your own well-being. And celebrate the control that you feel from having taken responsibility for self. Your soul will dance and sing. She is waiting for you to take back the reins of your life.

self-reflections

11

I AM ENOUGH

But am I? Am I enough? How can I believe this when others appear to be doing so much more, accomplishing so much more, earning so much more? I torture myself; thoughts racing through my consciousness, asking but knowing, deep down. "No, you are not." If you were, you would be getting more 'right,' accomplishing more, having wider impact, earning more money, and be more well-known. Abject misery creeps in, landing in the recesses of the mind. I breathe.

Am I a fraud, then? Do I not tell my clients and others that 'more' for the sake of More is not better? Am I being disingenuous when I proclaim that 'deeper' is better? Is it not true, then, that we *need* people to go deeper? Each one of us, in our own way, in whatever area sparks imagination and interest; each has the opportunity to drill down below the surface, below the façade of our lives. To get to the core, the deepest place of desire, the soul. To the place of personal soul-connectedness that generates personal authenticity. The authenticity that creates 'enough-ness,' the state of mind that repairs our state of being. And, is it not incumbent, now more than ever, to be in a repaired state of being?

The answer is Yes! Yes, to all! Yes, it is incumbent for each and every soul on earth to go deep, deeper still, to seek and find the core. To breathe and love and repair the cracks and the very sinew that runs through and holds together the body; to find your place of enough-ness. Be brave! Scratch your surface, find a crack, allow light to shine in. Do not be afraid of the light. Just allow the light to shine through, go deep and seep in. The only thing that will happen is that there will be light there! There will be light in your darkness if you allow it. Then, it is there in that place of repair, of healing that you can step out and shine. And in that light, you can know, you are enough.

Let us each take whatever responsibility we need to in order to claim enough-ness, to feel enough, to really know we are enough so that we can be the 'more' we seek. What, then, will you do with your enough-ness? What will you share, what light will you then shed for others, to light their way? Get clear, get confident, stand in your light; shine and lead. Our world needs you to feel enough, to be enough and to shine your personal light of impact.

self-reflections

12

I AM A HEALER

I used to feel worried and anxious about time passing. I had so much I wanted to do and accomplish that perseverated in my mind but it constantly clashed and conflicted with the life obligations and responsibilities I felt that seemed mundane; I yearned to be in the sacred. In that period of my life, I felt like I was under water with debris floating on the surface bumping and crashing together and preventing me from coming up for air, "What about me, what about me, what about me?"

When I think back now, I can feel the cold, murky dank closing in around me. I can feel the word "Help" on my lips, long and drawn-out, as I sink. But then, I just called that life. "It's just my way" I used to say to myself and others. I used to wonder, "Why didn't anyone help me? Why didn't anyone really see me

I am one who is ready and willing.

drowning? Why didn't anyone take my hand and help me rise?"

Today, I know the answer. It has been and continues to be revealed to me daily: "Through your struggle, you fought. From your struggle, you rose. Because of your struggle, your hand is offered. Easily, you reach to others; plunging your hand down into the dark, cold water, swiping aside the debris, finding fingers, clasping the hand and pulling up. You connect soul-to-soul. And you help heal, offering others soul-connection. This is your healing; you are a Healer."

It has taken me years, hundreds of hours, thousands of minutes, millions of seconds to accept. And still, surely, I question, can it be true? *Who am I to help heal?* Each time now, though, the answer comes to me easily. Who am I to help heal? I am one who is ready and willing. Willing to hold a hand in soul-connection not with answers, but with love. I have learned that confidence does not come from expertise and surface accomplishments. It comes from deep belief, in self, in love, in face, in mind, body, and from soul. I no longer have to be right, or to get it right every time. I just have to stay connected to my own soul (now, I have Tools for this)! And I radiate.

The biggest surprise was realizing that all of my earlier deep yearning for success, accomplishments, achievement, and recognition has become soothed with the same aging I used to fear! The passing of time has supported me! As I committed to getting onto a path of calm, of peace, and of joy, my mind quieted. I felt better and better and made more and more impact! Now, I see clearly that my aging has supported my personal growth, wisdom gleaned and gained, to be shared and spread through healing.

The passing of time, with my children grown and gone has allowed me to find my breath, open all of my senses to realize that my success with just one soul—in my coaching, training or in my courses—is more than good enough; it is full and complete. I accomplished and achieved daily what I thought I would never achieve in a lifetime. Offering one human healing through soul-to-soul connecting and their personal soul-connection is an entirely complete experience and achievement, each and every time. Full success in every moment. I no longer fear time passing. I no longer fear aging. My time is here and now. And when my time is over, I will be complete.

self-reflections

13

SOMETHING BIG IS COMING

Do you remember Excitement? The feeling of joy and giggles and butterflies in your stomach, when you had delicious anticipation of your birthday party or a big holiday coming? What happened to that buoyant feeling? When did Excitement turn to Anxiety for you? Was it when expectations were unmet? Was it when disappointments crept in? Was it when play turned to chores and obligations turned to overwhelm?

Anxiety can be the shadow side of Excitement. 'So much' as a child can turn to 'too much' as a young adult when there is already a lot evolving in your mind, body and soul. Is Anxiety, then, familiar to you? Whether or not you are diagnosed with a clinical mental health disorder, Anxiety can be an unwanted newcomer

Your child Soul prays for Excitement again.

within. Or, for some, the newcomer may have turned into the guest who never leaves. Can you see this picture? You feel Excitement about Something Big Coming and Excitement gets filled with questions, you get flooded with negative thoughts. Then Overwhelm draws dark curtains, your mind closes to Opportunity, Joy and Possibility, and you lose yourself. Can you feel the shrouded unrequited feeling?

You see it, feel it, shrug your shoulders and allow it to stay over there, just out of reach. But what if it was within reach? What if you stood up straight and tall, stretched out your arm in front of you as far as it could go, opened your hand wide and felt the tip of your fingers touch it? What if, when you touch it, you breathe and throw back the curtains? What if the light begins to flood in and you feel a spark sizzle up your arm, travel throughout your body and shock your heart? What if you give yourself permission to feel Excitement again, to discover your authentic you? Something Big is Coming.

Don't fear it. Don't block it. Don't stay behind the dark, drawn curtains. You're on the stage behind the curtain, head down praying, butterflies inciting, "Is it my turn now?" Breathe deeply, oxygenate your internal systems, stand up straight and tall, reach out both of your arms in front of you—as far as they can go—open your hands wide and feel the spark. Curtain up! Fear not, feel Excited. Something Big is Coming.

Awe can be the light side of Excitement. But 'Awe,' you say? That's not for me. I'm not saintly. I'm not larger than life, or better than anyone else or even truly better than my own thoughts allow. But Awe can be for you if you breathe deeply, get quiet inside and listen. Feel the stirrings of your child Soul. Breathe again, get quieter still and listen even more deeply. Your child Soul prays for Excitement again. Help her throw back the dark curtains, feel the spark, jump for Joy, imagine the Possibilities and know Awe. Dig deep. Find your Truth. Choose, decide, commit now. Something Big is Coming. Step out and let Awe in.

self-reflections

14

THE ARMY OF CHANGE

Are you feeling invisible? Are you feeling that your middle-aged self, your body, your face, even your mind are not valued by those around you, possibly even the people in your own family? I see this sentiment expressed repeatedly in social media discussion threads of large women's groups. I can see these groups have become a lifeline for many. A safe space to ask embarrassing questions, to share feelings and emotions about this time of life where, blessedly, judgment is usually limited and love is often abundant. As such, I read endless comments from women in midlife feeling unvalued and unseen. In my coaching work with women in the second half of life, I hear similar sentiments.

After a recent experience supporting my 91-year-

See yourself for who you are, now.

old father in rehabilitation at a nursing home, I just want to scream. I feel rage building inside, barely able to contain it when others complain endlessly, not seeing what their lives might otherwise be. Stop whining! Stop complaining about being unseen and see yourself! You are stellar in every way. You are vital, smart, and beyond the worry of other's opinions. You have skills and life experience to share and can impact our world in ways beyond your imagination. And, the stakes are high.

Stop whining! Stop complaining. Each and every one of us must get to work. Right now, the time is now. It is not hyperbole to say the stakes are higher than ever. The world is literally melting from climate change and we are worried about not being seen by men when we walk into a car dealership?

See yourself! Value yourself more. Accept and embrace your unique value proposition as a woman who can nurture, manage, and accomplish. Isn't that exactly what you've done for decades? Accomplished more than you could have imagined, caring for self, families, pets, work, church, community, partners, parents, and more!

See yourself for who you are, now. Each and every one of us must step outside our comfort zone if that's what it takes. Get clear and confident of your own skills and abilities and walk into any agency that serves, present yourself, and get to work as a volunteer. If you need paid work, then get your resume in order, cross-train with others, get comfortable speaking your message, realize the transference of your skills and confidently charge the value of your worth. We must do this and we must persist, no matter what! We have decades ahead of us to create change that is desperately needed for our children and grandchildren's healthy future.

We must step outside our comfort zone. We must see ourselves and stop waiting to be seen by anyone else. We must come out from behind our curtains of shame because our bodies are expanding or our faces are wrinkled. We must expose ourselves for the skills and talents we have, beyond the ability for others to understand. Let them underestimate us. Let us be the army of change. Let us stand up, *see ourselves*, get seen and heard and fight. We must, the time is now.

self-reflections

15

GET CONTROL OF YOUR MIND

How are you at getting control of your mind? If you wonder, with curiosity not judgment, if you take a few breaths and quiet your inner self, what are the thoughts that you hear? When you come to conscious awareness, what are the thoughts that swirl around your mind? Are they thoughts of worry, anxiousness, concerns, challenges, fears? If you are honest with yourself, it is easy to realize that these are the types of thoughts that shower over us most of the time.

In this day and age, there is so much going on around us externally, dive-bombing us nearly every moment, that it is hard to not react. It is hard to stay contained and not respond. But it is in your best interest to figure out how to get control of your mind. When you wake up in the morning and pick up your

It is more important than ever for you to get control of your mind.

phone before your eyes are even fully open, before you even take that conscious awake breath, you are being bombarded with everything that's happening around the globe, most of which is so far out of your control. When you subject yourself to that onslaught it is impossible for your mind and even your physical body to not react or respond in a negative way.

Perhaps it is true that the ills of the world have always been there, since the beginning of humankind. But the exposure to every single thing, in every single moment has not always been there. It is vitally important for you to consider how you choose to be confronted when affronted with that bombardment. It is equally important for you to consider how you choose to respond or react and for you to figure out what is in your control versus what is not in your control.

In this time, on this day, at this moment it is more important than ever for you to get control of your mind. It is more important than ever for you to use all of your senses and your sensibility to find your calm when all around you rage rages. Any one of us who takes the personal responsibility to get conscious, get clear, and get calm will be a balm to the world. It is true that each of us is an entire universe. Each of us, a world that intersects with the next human universe, the world of any person clashing up against another.

If I take my personal responsibility to find my calm place, my physical appearance and persona and my energy will positively impact that of the next person and so on and so on. Just as the rage inside one affects and leads to the rage inside another. It is a choice to get control of your mind, to quiet your own thoughts, to be in awareness of who you want to be and how you want to be. It is your choice to lead life positively. You choose.

self-reflections

16

YOUR SOUL, UNIQUELY YOURS

What is truly unique anymore in our world? Do you ever feel that way? You look around and think, "It's all been done before. What is left for me to do? I can't really invent, discover or create anything new." I beg to differ. You know what is unique? Your soul, and your energy. Never before and never again duplicated. Understand this, and you will see/learn what is yours to create, what is yours to give. Yours, all yours.

Take time to reflect, to explore the characteristics that make up you. What is that thing you do that people always respond to by saying, "Thank you" (for listening, for sharing, for teaching, for helping)! What is it that you say or do that people resonate and respond to with appreciation, with awe (if you see it), with a

Take time to reflect, to explore the characteristics that make up you.

synergistic enthusiasm? Think about this, consider it—is it an experience you offer, is it a feeling in them that you create? Where does it come from in you? Is it 'just there' for you, no fabrication or thinking required?

If you find yourself saying, "I just don't know what it is" then go deeper, explore more. Self-reflect, refine your lens and review your filter. Give yourself permission to shine—imagine the possibility that there is something special in you that is unique. There is! Your DNA, your soul, your energy.

Why is it important to understand this? Because it is the answer you seek to the soul-questions you ask yourself consciously or subconsciously: What is my purpose? What am I intended to do in my life/with my life? What impact am I intended to make while in the world? And this one, eventually and inevitably: What will my legacy be?

Mostly, our soul stays buried deep down inside, huddled below the crap and chaos of our lives. The 'stuff' of life that we create to deny or avoid the feeling of intensity around what I call soul-agenda. It is intense. When you excavate down and finetune your understanding of your unique soul, the place of deepest feeling that shines like an exquisite multi-faceted diamond in you, you connect. You connect to feeling, to impact. With an intensity born of knowing your purpose, being on-purpose; knowing your life-plan all in real-time. It is 'a lot' to handle if you haven't done the work. The work involves breathing, clearing, stretching out the body that is constantly hunched, opening up the pathways and imagining. 'What If' my soul is unique? What, then? What is it that my soul is intended to offer? How can I learn, what can I do to unleash this unique offering? Am I ready? Do I want this?

Don't be afraid; finding your soul's uniqueness offers comfort, confidence and calm. You don't have to 'do' anything, you can just 'be.' Consider this, do the work, feel the impact and the results will come pouring out of you easily, organically and with more power than your mind can currently conceive. If you do this, then not only will you be able to conceive of it, but you will believe in it. And, in yourself.

self-reflections

17

LET GO

What if you let go? What would happen? Would everything fall apart?

What are you holding onto? Is it anger, is it sadness, resentment, worry, fear? Can you identify it? What you hold onto, holds on to you. Fear not. It works both ways! If you hold onto good, to love, to caring, to kind, to compassion, to Joy, to peace then that holds on to you!

But mostly, we hold on to the bad, the negative thoughts and ideas that race through our mind; it's a conversation we are having with ourselves constantly. You may not realize it but often that is what's going on in the background of your mind, holding on to the bad.

You may think active overt thoughts of "I want it to be different," "I don't want it to be like this," "why this," "why that," "why not me." But those thoughts all focus

Let go of the "No" that you tell yourself, replace it with "Yes."

on the exact thing that is. The thing you want to let go of. Do you realize this? Can you see this, that you give the negative thoughts the most precious real estate in you? Why do we do this? How does it serve to hold on? How would it serve to let go?

Let go of the "No" that you tell yourself, replace it with "Yes." "Yes, I can." And "Yes, I will." "Yes, I am." And "Yes, it is for me." Create, grow, and enhance these thoughts and plant them repeatedly until they are implanted and working as the background support to create the life you want to live. Yes, you can; yes, it's possible. Let go of the negative things that have become comfortable, familiar, even deeply ingrained in your life.

You might be surprised at the process of letting go. This process might evoke tears, confusion, even anxiety. This happens in transition, with change. Use your breath to 'clear' and find tools to create the new way of being that you want to feel. Ask yourself the seminal soul-connection two-part question: "Who do I want to be and how do I want to be?" Explore the options of tools readily available: journal, pray, meditate, create, sing, be in nature, or just breathe. Breathe In and Out. Allow your breath to support the quieting of your mind. Ask yourself questions, answer "Yes" every time; let go of "No." Imagine this. Feel what it feels like.

Letting go of the 'No' in life is precious. Saying yes to the success that you envision is Sublime. Say "Yes" to feeling. Say "Yes" to soul. Say "Yes" to love. Say "Yes" to living out loud, in comfort, in calm, in joy. LET GO of everything else. Say, "Yes."

self-reflections

BONUS MEDITATION

Soul Rising

This meditation is powerful if you give it full permission to serve you. Take a moment now to breathe in deeply, and exhale slowly. Take a few more deep breaths and consciously let your shoulders down. Relax your body.

She's in there. Your soul. Yes, she's in there. Deep down.

And, she wants to Rise. She yearns to Rise; to leave the darkness where she has been pushed, shoved, dismissed and ignored, and return to the light. Not the eternal gold-light of the heavens, but the bright clear blue-light of the day. This day. In this moment.

Her path up from the depths starts with a breath. Your breath. Deep and enduring. Now, take a deep breath in and a long breath out. And again, deep breath in and long breath out. And keep breathing, easily now.

This breath helps you clear the path up for her. At once, gentle and calm while also cutting ruthlessly like a

The power is in you. Yes, the power is in you.

machete through the clutter and chaos, or darkness and depression that has convened in your body, created by sacred wounds of the past; captured now and lying dormant, each and every one unsettled, fearsome, boiling, palpable if you dare go near it.

Mostly, the obstructions just sit there, weeds from them growing down deep, strong, thick embedding in your subconsciousness and holding tightly to the genesis.

It is your breath that is your own natural weapon, your very own breath is the warrior you seek. This warrior is gentle, it is persistent, ever-present, ever-able and always victorious! Always on duty and ready to serve, when you are ready to win. Ready to win over darkness, sadness, depression, anxiety, and apathy.

Your breath is the chariot upon which the Amazon Soul in you rides. In this chariot, you have strength not previously imagined.

The power is in you. Yes, the power is in you.

Not docile, not tranquil, not impotent, the power of your soul to Rise is fierce, unexpected and it is in your control. In your control.

Your soul is your power, your power is your soul. She is activated by your breath, your desire to be free, to feel agile, to let go of the dark and rise to the light. Swimming, swimming, swimming up, up, up. Batting away obstruction, slashing at the barriers, slicing through resistance, swimming, swimming higher still, rising toward the light. Up through your core, clearing out your lungs, piercing through your heart, she rises. Higher and higher through your throat giving you Voice, pulling the shades from your eyes as she rises and suddenly you see the clear violet and blue tones, you can see the light; it's there for the reaching, for the wanting.

Ahead of you the crown, the Keter, pulling you in, drawing you up higher and faster still. Knowing! It is yours. Yours for the reaching, for the wanting. Certainty. Trust. Truth.

You crash through the surface, gasping for air, you-have-arrived. Your soul has arrived! She is there, there in the light.

You, in the light.

Soul Rising.

CONCLUSION

Self-Reflections, What Now?

Dear Friend,

I started the introduction of this book with "Dear Reader."

Now, after our journey together through these pages, I call you Friend.

So Friend, what now? Hopefully, you have taken time for yourself, time to read, reflect, write and share with others these positive thoughts and ideas. Now, how will you keep them integrated into your life and apply them daily? This is important because continued self-reflection is where soul-connection lies. Continued commitment to self, being aware of the thoughts you think —if/how/when— what does this look like for you?

How will you turn your self-reflection into the

action you want in order to live your Vision of life in your second half? Soul-connection is part of the answer. When your soul is soothed, when she feels seen and heard, she rises. When your soul rises, that's when you feel confident, clear and calm, like you're on-purpose and on-point, and that's when the passion kicks in. When you wake up daily, are grateful for your breath, for your life and feel ready to step up and step out; you will feel in control of your life—possibly for the first time in your life.

I hope your self-reflection leads you to your own Call to Action: What's it going to take? For you to step up, step out and live the life you want, the life of your *dreams*. And...be easy on yourself. You don't have to leap-there-now, you can just begin to move in that direction and go forward and forward and forward. What would you have told your younger self? "Appreciate the journey," no?

This book is yours, it will be there for whatever you need to revisit in its pages. Use it to support you on the path.

Please stay in touch.

With love,

Susan

WITH SUCH GRATITUDE

To my clients. I am grateful for your trust, for your commitment to the 'work' together, for showing up for me as the Coach and way more importantly, for showing up for you. I have watched, learned and gleaned the power of self-reflection from our work.

And to countless others, friends, relatives, acquaintances, colleagues, strangers on a plane, bus or train, I am grateful for the conversation we've had together. In which you somehow went in deeply so quickly and shared your soul's burdens or desires with me. I was happy to listen. I learned so much from you, from your courage to engage in that authentic way with me. I feel humbled by this and grateful for my own journey that led me to the place of being able to get still, stay quiet and listen.

And still there are others, those who participated in my soul-connecting visualizations. Permitting me to go into my intuitive place in order to help you 'see,' to envision your reality, the future you so deeply desire. Thank you for allowing me to experience this with you and for showing me that this is how I show up as a healer. I am grateful.

ABOUT THE AUTHOR

Susan Axelrod, CCP, is the go-to Confidence Coach for Women. Specializing in working with executive women and matriarchs in mid-life who have spent decades doing for others... IT'S YOUR TURN NOW. What does 'my turn' look like? Using co-creative & co-facilitative coaching methods, Susan helps clients uncover the inspired soul within who is looking to live out the second half of life in a self-fulfilling and purposeful way. Susan doesn't give answers or advice. She works with clients to dig into their core, to explore the girl she was and the woman she wants to be for the rest of her life, personally, professionally, spiritually and physically. Using original Confident-Life ™ Tools, Susan helps women find the Clarity and Confidence they seek to live out a *Best Life*. She works with women in transition who declare themselves 'READY!' ...ready to GROW, ready to LIVE now and create a meaningful and lasting legacy. Susan's contagious enthusiasm and deep listening skills sparks and motivates clients to get Confident and Thrive!

Susan's Motivational Speaking and online and in-person Confident-Life Workshops™ are a hit every time! Available for work-teams, book clubs, friend groups, women CEO clubs, nonprofits or any place women gather.

Certified Coach Practitioner, through The Coach Training Academy [accredited by the International Coaching Federation and Certified Coaches Alliance].

CONNECT WITH SUSAN

Confident-Life™
Imagine the Possibilities.

Are you ready to live a more Confident-Life™?

Contact Susan now, you'll be glad you did.

When you call, Susan responds.
Everything is timely, 100% personal and 100% custom.

Connect personally with Susan for coaching, bring her in to do a Confident-Life Workshop™ or as a Motivational Speaker for your group.

CONTACT:
susan@confident-life.com | 518-495-4573

**Here's the down-&-dirty list to find me,
I truly love to connect personally with my readers.
I look forward to 'seeing you' anywhere!**

Look me up on FB or LinkedIn by my name, Susan Axelrod!

Here's my FB biz page: 'What Will Your Legacy Be?'

Here's my FB group: 'Discovering You Again'

Here's my website: www.whatwillyourlegacybe.com

My body of work lives on my YouTube Channel: The Confidence Zone with Coach Susan Axelrod

And, of course, find me on Amazon, Author name- Susan Lowenthal Axelrod

TESTIMONIALS

"In only a few calls with Susan as my coach, through her effectively listening, she has provided several tools to help me lead with integrity - and enhance my inner confidence. Hiring Susan to coach me was a solid investment I made in myself. Grateful that I made the commitment to hire her. She helps me see and think differently - and lead with confidence."
-Gloria J., Nonprofit Executive

"Susan, I watch you 'LIVE' and feel uplifted, inspired and educated during these dark days.. Thank you for helping me consider possibilities, please know you have an impact. Most people are careful, you are brave and noisy and hopeful. Right now, we need change. Careful doesn't cause change. Thank you for helping us all feel more confident to live the life we want. Keep shining."
-Julie Richmond Blackburn

"You are such a BIG hearted source of support. I admire you and the work you do." ... "I can say this, the world needs more generous-hearted people like Susan. We're all better for knowing her, so I can't recommend checking out her program enough!"
-Carol Egan, High Performance Health Coach at carol-egan.com

"What I love about you, Susan, is that you appear in your authenticity to be fearless, that's how I see you. I see you taking fearless action to be authentic to your vision and to be authentic to your dreams, your work and what it is that you teach. I know as a master coach, myself, that we come up against our own limiting beliefs during the time when we take big risks and big action. We come up against our own limitations but I see you moving beyond those limitations at the speed of light. I see you on the leading edge of being out there in the world, teaching and leading, and showing what's possible when we play full out."
-Kornelia Stephanie, Media Entrepreneur, Coach, Healer, Speaker at korneliastephanie.com